PUFFIN BOOKS

THE I-HATE-SCHOOL S

CONGRATULATIONS!

The mere fact that you've picked this book up and opened it means that you are seriously interested in SCHOOL – or how to survive it. Whether you love or hate it, the truth is that you're likely to spend at least twelve years of your life in school, so you might as well get the most out of it.

This hilarious A–Z of school life will show you how to do lots of things, including how to make the most of your zits, how to forge realistic sick-notes, how to really enjoy museum visits and how to drive your teacher crazy, as well as introducing you to lots of new and useful words that your parents and teachers will never understand.

WARNING – DON'T SHOW THIS BOOK TO YOUR PARENTS. IT MIGHT MAKE THEM WANT TO RETURN TO SCHOOL.

Sebastian Spottly-Bott and Kylie Klunkit are the hugely talented pair that first introduced the world to the 'brown-and-soggy-banana-skin-in-other-kids'-pockets-and-kitbags-when-they're-out-playing-games' joke. It quickly caught on and sales of brown and soggy bananas shot up. Since then, Seb and Kylie have been inundated with requests from publishers to write down their school experiences. Puffin are delighted to be publishing this book, although it cost them an arm and a leg (and millions of brown and soggy bananas).

The I-Hate-School Survival Guide

PUFFIN BOOKS

PUFFIN BOOKS

Published by the Penguin Group
Penguin Books Ltd, 27 Wrights Lane, London W8 5TZ, England
Penguin Books USA Inc., 375 Hudson Street, New York, New York 10014, USA
Penguin Books Australia Ltd, Ringwood, Victoria, Australia
Penguin Books Canada Ltd, 10 Alcorn Avenue, Toronto, Ontario, Canada M4V 3B2
Penguin Books (NZ) Ltd, 182–190 Wairau Road, Auckland 10, New Zealand

Penguin Books Ltd, Registered Offices: Harmondsworth, Middlesex, England

First published 1992
10 9 8 7 6 5 4 3

Text copyright © Complete Editions, 1992
Illustrations copyright © Alan Rowe, 1992
All rights reserved

The moral right of the author has been asserted

Printed in England by Clays Ltd, St Ives plc
Filmset in Lasercomp Rockwell

Dear Reader,

When we were asked to write this book we
thought the publishers were mad, but – come to
think of it – there's no one better qualified than us
to give the low-down on how to survive at school.
Between us we've served more than fifteen years
in the class-room, so we're hardened and
desperate school-kids!

Sebastian is currently at St Cuthbert's. He's
previously escaped from Eaton and Harrough and
he's already planning to get expelled yet again. I
go to Bulldozer High School, which is so totally
horrible that no one ever gets kicked out, worst
luck.

We met in the back seat of the Pirate Ship ride
at Chessington World of Adventure last summer.
It was hate-at-first-sight, but when we were both
sick over everyone else at the same moment we
knew there was something special between us.
And when I found Sebastian had just eaten two
plates of chips, four doughnuts, three chocolate
milk shakes, a pound of kola kubes and a passion-
fruit ice-cream, I felt certain we were made for

each other – cos that's exactly what I'd had for lunch too.

To work on this book we had to take a few weeks off school. I managed it by biting a Rottweiler and faking rabies. Sebastian staged a fall from his polo pony and pretended to break his legs. Brilliant excuses, aren't they?

Anyway, this book is full of all the things we've learnt at school over the last few years. No, not maths and geografy and technology, you idiot! We mean *really* useful stuff that'll help you survive at school and maybe even have a few laughs!

We've had lots of fun writing this book, and we would have had a lot more if the publisher hadn't asked a horrible teacher to keep an eye on the contents. But we know you're not going to take any notice of what teacher says, because it's a load of rubbish. (*What was that? Did you say something, Kylie? Teacher.*)

See what I mean? Anyway, see you around the playground some time. And remember – never wash, never volunteer and wear protective clothing when you're handling school gravy!

Bye!
Kylie

An A–Z of School Life

Acne

You've got acne? Ha-ha-ha! Hello, Liverface! What's it like to have oozing pustules exploding all over your cheeks? (*Stop these insults at once! Teacher.*)

Er, well, seriously, acne is a brilliant thing to have. Unlike ordinary spots, which everybody gets, only the coolest people get acne. Some people who only have a few measly zits go round *pretending* they've got acne. So congratulations if you've got the real thing. Fester with pride!

If you really, really can't bear it, go to the doctor, who may give you some antibiotics to try and clear it up. Unlike other spots, acne isn't helped much by using the face-washes and lotions you can buy over the counter. If nothing works, bad luck. You'll just have to put up with the spots until you grow out of them. It doesn't matter what it looks like, honest. And remember, you can threaten anyone who laughs at you by pointing your biggest, most volcanic zit in their direction and threatening to squeeze it at them. That should shut 'em up!

If you've got acne do not, on any account, do these things:

- Scrape your spots off with the electric sander in the school workshop.
- Go to bed, pull up the cover and stay there for the next five years.
- Wear a Balaclava helmet until you are twenty-one.
- Fill the craters in your skin with Polyfilla and give yourself two coats of Flesh Pink gloss paint.

Also worth looking up SPOTS and ZITS.

Acting

Forget all those stupid old actors prancing round the stage doing cissy Shakespeare! Forget the Oscars! No, Bruce Willis and the *Home and Away* crew don't know what real acting is because they've never seen Elvis Sidebottom of Catstrangler Middle School do his famous 'I'll cut off my feet in remorse' speech when he's caught wearing trainers in the class-room.

Acting is the first thing you need to learn at school. In fact it's the *only* thing you need to learn at school, cos once you can act you can do anything. The most important bits of acting you need to get right are:

1. Saying, 'It wasn't me, miss,' when it was.
2. Acting innocent.

A few tips from us, who are both brilliant actors and have taught the *Grange Hill* kids everything we know. Pity they didn't listen to us!

To begin with, it helps if you don't blush, burst into tears, stare at your feet or faint when you're acting. This is a dead give-away. Even the dimmest teacher will suspect you're acting if you say, 'No, miss, it wasn't me who drew that picture of you being trampled by a herd of buffalo on the board,' and then go bright red and burst into tears. You can practise at home by standing in front of a mirror and telling the biggest porkies you can think of with a straight face. If you can say, 'Sebastian's sister is the most beautiful girl in the world,' without laughing, you're doing OK.

Acting innocent is more difficult. If you look innocent it's easier, so try to look like the kind of wimpy kid who never does anything wrong. Keep your pellet-gun, assassination diary and any other incriminating evidence hidden in a shiny brief-case. Cover up your tattoos with a nice clean plaster. Brush your teeth once a week. You know the kind of thing teachers like. Once you're disguised as an innocent wimp, you can do practically anything you want, as long as you don't look as if you're doing it. Got that? Good.

Also worth looking up DRAMA.

Armpits

Never, ever wash your armpits, that's our advice.
We once heard of a girl who washed hers and
they shrank, so we're not taking any risks. One
advantage of having grungy, mega-smelly armpits
like ours is that we don't have to put our hands
up in class any more. Teachers prefer us to sit at
the back doing nothing rather than putting up our
hands to answer questions and filling the class-
room with noxious fumes! Brilliant, innit?
Also worth looking up BOOTS and FEET.

Art

Our favourite art class is working with clay. We
make lots of really horrible things with lumps
sticking out all over them and paint them
disgusting colours like puke-green and snot-
yellow. At Christmas we give these wickedly nasty
items as presents to our grannies and other
wrinklies, and they have to say, 'Oh, what a lovely
green ashtray with bits sticking out of it. Did you
make it yourself, you brilliant child?' Then they
have to put it on the mantelpiece.

A few days after Christmas this work of art will
probably disappear and your granny will pretend
she doesn't know what happened to it. Try looking
in the dustbin. If you find it there, cry and scream
and say that you made it specially for her. She'll
feel so guilty that she'll buy you something nice to
make up for being so utterly ungrateful.

Other things worth learning in art are silk-
screen printing and forging. Get your teacher to

10

show you how to silk-screen T-shirts. This is
brilliant, because once you know how you can
silk-screen tasteful T-shirts with slogans like 'Mrs
Nutter never uses loo-paper' or 'Bad spellers of
the world – untie' and sell them for loadsamoney
to your mates. Forging is a bit more difficult, but
it can be very rewarding. Class 3C at Bulldozer
High bought themselves Porsches with the money
they made during Mr Willie's art lessons. Then
the police caught up with them and now Mr
Willie's in jail. But don't worry, sir, we're making
£20 notes now and when you come out you'll be a
rich man!

Art Galleries

There are three good reasons for going on school trips to art galleries. First, they're big places and it's very easy to get lost in them. Second, they're full of pictures of people with no clothes on, which is always good for a giggle. Third, there's usually a café in them, so you can get some good scoff. **Also worth looking up MUSEUMS and OUTINGS.**

Assassination

Assassination is the last resort when things get seriously tough at school. If there's a kid or a teacher who's making life difficult and you've tried everything else to get them off your back, you might eventually have to take out a contract on them. (*I'm not sure I like the sound of this. Teacher.*)

We've done it ourselves a few times. Miss Spriggly, Sebastian's infant-school teacher, met a sticky end when she made him stop reading *Pulverizer Meets the Dragon Woman* and try *Ronald the Rabbit Goes Shopping* instead. (*Miss Spriggly? Miss Spriggly of Wellbrungup Mixed Infants? The Miss Spriggly who drowned mysteriously in a giant pot of paste? Teacher.*)

The most difficult thing about organizing an assassination is finding the school assassin. Assassins don't want to be recognized, otherwise their victims would run away when they saw them coming. So they're always in disguise, usually as the total wimp everyone hates. The only way to check whether someone is the school assassin is to whisper these code words at them: 'Why don't you go home? Your cage should have been cleaned out by now.'

If the person is the school assassin they will say, 'Give me the time, the place and the victim.' If they aren't the school assassin they will probably hit you over the head with their brief-case. This is why you should use assassination only as a last resort. Finding the assassin can be a difficult and painful job. (*This is a joke, isn't it? Isn't it? Stop mucking about, you two. Teacher.*)

Of course it's only a joke, Teacher. Isn't it, readers . . . ?

Also worth looking up DEATH.

Assembly

We're talking mega-zzzzzz time here, aren't we, friends? Two bits of advice on how to cope with it:

1. Assembly usually involves religion of some kind, so join a religious cult that bans its members from attending other religious gatherings. If you have difficulty finding one, you can join ours. It's called the Church of the Latter Day Truants and all you have to do is send £500 in used notes to K. Klunkit at Bulldozer High. We'll send you a letter saying you are excused from assembly and you'll never have to go again!

2. If you can't get out of it, join in. Yes, that's right. Sing the songs as loud as you can. Listen while your head teacher makes stupid and cringy remarks about loving each other and nod vigorously all the time. Stand up at the end and thank the head for leading such a brilliant assembly. It won't be long before they take you gently off to the sick-bay and make you lie down for half an hour before sending you home. **Also worth looking up BUNKING OFF.**

Bananas

We don't usually eat any fruit or veg because they're supposed to be good for us, but bananas are different. Not only does the middle bit taste nice, but you can do brilliant things with the skins. For example, keep banana skins in your desk until they go brown and soggy, then nip into the gym changing-rooms while everyone's out playing football and put bits in people's shoes and pockets

14

and at the bottom of their bags. Yeurrgh!

Always take a banana with you on school outings. For best results, also take egg sandwiches. After half an hour on the coach, when everyone's feeling a bit sicky-wicky, have a smelly egg sandwich followed by a smelly banana. Pass the sick bags, Teacher!

Bikes

There are two types of bike. First, there's *the* bike, which is OK. Second, there's the wally bike, which is not OK.

The bikes are basically twenty-gear mountain bikes, but you'll also be OK with a really good racing bike. Nothing else will do.

Wally bikes include all of the following: BMXs you were given for Christmas three years ago; your mum's 'shopper' bike; your dad's fold-up bike with wheels the size of 10p pieces; your big sister's pink girly bike; your kid brother's Mutant Hero Teenage Turtles tricycle; any other bike.

The big problem with having *the* bike is that everyone else wants it too. Including us. It's no good just locking it up, because if we really want to borrow it we'll saw through a lamp-post to get it. So if you've got one, don't ride it. Hang it up on your bedroom wall and think how lucky you are to own something so amazingly wonderful.

If you've got a wally bike you don't have to worry about locking it up because no one in their right mind would nick it. Good news, eh? The bad news is that you look a total plonker when you're riding it. Oh, don't start crying! (*Now look what you've done. Teacher.*)

Boarding-school
Boarding-school is brilliant because you don't have to see your mum and dad for weeks and you live with a big gang of other kids. Boarding-schools would be perfect if it wasn't for the teachers, but no one takes any notice of teachers anyway. (*What was that? Did you say something? Teacher.*)

Sebastian has been to seven boarding-schools and been expelled from five of them, including Eaton and Harrough, so he is a real expert. The worst was Och-I-the-noo Secure School in Scotland.

All the boys had to wear kilts and go for a swim in freezing Loch Ness every morning, and there was nothing to eat except cold porridge. To escape, he had to cross a minefield, pole-vault over a pit of burning oil and walk thirty miles in snow until his kneecaps froze and fell off.

His favourite boarding-school was St Muffin's, which was a 'progressive' school. The teachers believed that kids didn't have to do lessons if they didn't want to, so they didn't. Sebastian wanted to stay there for ever, but unfortunately the school didn't feel the same about him after the teachers found soggy bananas in the tea-bag jar.

Bogies

Bogies make lovely presents for people. We always try to leave a few on our desks, so the next kid to sit there finds them. What a lovely surprise, ha-ha! We sometimes send bogies to our unfavourite teachers, too. We rub them over our books and work, so that . . . (*Yeeeugh?! What's this slimy stuff on your maths homework, Spottly-Bott? Don't tell me it's a – aaaaaagh! You disgusting child! Teacher.*)

Boots

Rugby boots, football boots, hockey boots – whatever kind of boots you wear for sport, you should treat them all in the same way. Never,

ever clean them. If you do they'll turn vicious and start kicking people. Teachers and mums don't know this, so tell them we told you so. Never clean out the insides or use Odour-eaters or you'll kill all those lovely, pongy bacteria that live in them. David Attenborough's planning to do a whole series on the wildlife living inside Kylie's PE plimsolls!

By the end of term, with a bit of luck, you'll be able to get out of games because no one will be able to stand within 100 metres of your boots without fainting from the smell. Now it's time to call in the Ultra-Dangerous Toxic Waste Disposal experts, who will take your boots away and bury them a mile underground, where they can't do any damage to the environment. All you have to do is go home and tell your mum you've lost them and need a new pair. Easy-peasy, isn't it?
Also worth looking up ARMPITS and ENVIRONMENT.

Boring
School is boring. Lessons are boring. Homework is boring. Teachers are boring. Anything your mum says is 'nice' is boring. Anything you don't want to do is boring. Being a kid is boring. Being a grown-up is *really* boring. The Pet Shop Boys are mega-boring, even if they say they aren't. Got that?

It's a rule of school life that you have to say 'boring' at least fifty times a day. It drives the wrinklies wild. So when a teacher asks why you haven't done your work, you say, 'Because it's boring, sir.' It makes them mad, because they *know* it's true! Yeahhh!

The other thing to remember is that *you* must never, ever be boring. But you never are, are you, dear reader?

Bottom Burps

A bottom burp is usually known as a four-letter word beginning with F and ending with T, but because this is a rude word we've been banned from using it. Bottom burp is a polite way of putting it. (*Not very polite, if you ask me. Teacher.*)

Some people have a talent for bottom burps. Sebastian can do really disgusting ones that are so bad people have to wear gas masks. One famous bottom burper is Tracy Simmonds of Bulldozer High, who can produce terrible silent smells that knock out anyone standing next to her. She once f**rted during assembly and 200 people had to go to hospital. She's now known as Smelly Simmonds and works for the local council, fumigating buildings without any equipment!

Next time a teacher tells you off, do a strategic bottom burp. By the time the windows have been opened and everyone has started breathing again, they will have forgotten what they were doing. (*Silly kids! I always carry a clothes-peg to put on my nose, just in case! Teacher.*)

If you can't manage a truly deadly bottom burp, then try this recipe – it should produce a powerful result. Mix two large tins of baked beans with an extra-hot curry and a packet of All-Bran and swallow in ten seconds flat. Follow it with a two-litre bottle of fizzy drink. Jump up and down a bit. Wait an hour and then you should be ready to fire!

Once you get the hang of bottom-burp chemistry, you can create some really spectacular pongs. A combination of peanuts, cabbage and beans produces what's known as a 'silent killer'. Lentils, eggs and Brussels sprouts make a 'stonker'.

Sniff-sniff. Yeeeugh! Who did that? *You?* It's disgusting – congratulations!

Bullies

Bullies are big kids who gang up on little kids cos they're too scared to pick on someone their own size. We're no angels, but we've been picked on by bullies and we hate them because they're such cowards. Some kids turn into bullies because they're bullied at home by their parents. Others are just stupid and pick on other kids to make themselves feel important.

What should you do if you're being bullied? There are three ways of coping with bullying:

1. Give in. This is what a lot of kids do, because when a bully says, 'If you tell anyone what's happening, I'll murder you,' they believe them! You can usually tell which kids have given in to bullies. They cry all the time and won't go anywhere in the school on their own. This is sad, cos although school's a boring sort of place it shouldn't be *that* bad.

2. Get them. If there's a whole load of kids being bullied and you can get together and defend yourselves against the bully, this can work out. But remember, there's always going to be a day when you bump into the bully on your own and there's no one around to help you out . . .

3. Tell on them. Yeah, we know what the bully says. If you tell, you're a total wimp and he'll do something horrible to you. Get outta here! Tell everyone, and tell them loudly. Tell your form teacher, your favourite teacher, your mum and dad and all your friends. Don't be embarrassed, be brave. If you tell, you'll save other kids from

being as unhappy as you are. We'd tell. After all, school's 'orrible enough without having to put up with being bullied as well.

Also worth looking up ASSASSINATION.

Bunking Off

Bunking off is great, innit? Hanging around in the park on a cold winter afternoon when you could be in a nice warm class-room snoozing through geografy? Getting chucked out of the shopping centre when you could be doing something silly in art? Sitting at home watching daytime TV and discovering how to make a woolly tea-cosy for the 327th time? You're right – bunking off is boring.

These days we can't be bothered to bunk off. And when we overheard a teacher saying he was glad kids bunked off because it made his life much easier, that made our minds up. We're not having any of that! What do these teachers think they're getting paid for? To sit around in the staff-room doing nothing all day because their class has made a run for it?

So now, unless it's something really excruciating like double physics, we make life hell for them by turning up in class. Brilliant wheeze, eh, chaps?

Buses

Our favourite time of day comes around 3.30 p.m. when there's a massive bundle at the bus-stop. There's nothing like that incredible moment of triumph as we Rugby tackle our way through the

crowd and dangle from the handrails by our toes.
Yeah!

There are two serious problems with buses.
They are the driver and the other passengers. The
driver and the other passengers are always more
than 100 years old and hate kids. We have a
theory that the bus company pays some people to
sit on the bus all day just so they can moan at us.

We know that buses are for doing dares and
mucking about with your friends. I mean, what's
wrong with hanging by your fingertips out of the
top-deck windows? Or seeing how strong the seats
are by getting everyone in class 3C to sit on one
at the same time?

The other problem with buses is the school bus, which is used just for getting kids to school. Have you noticed that these buses are always the oldest, grottiest ones in the entire universe? It's not fair. Why can't we go to school in a brand-new bus with a video and a toilet? What do they think we are – animals?

Capital Punishment

Capital punishment is illegal but there are a few teachers who wouldn't mind seeing it brought back. They think that the occasional beheading on the games field would stop kids from dropping litter or running in the corridors. We think this is going ever-so-slightly over the top. (*Well, they might have a point . . . Teacher.*)
Also worth looking up CORPORAL PUNISHMENT and DEATH.

Caretakers

We spotted this advert for a school caretaker in the paper the other day:

> WANTED. Dozy old person to be
> CARETAKER at Bulldozer High. The
> right person must be bad-tempered,
> rude and unable to remember
> anything for more than three minutes.
> Skills in losing keys, yelling, 'You
> can't do that here,' and shambling
> around in a brown coat required.

When we grow up, we're going to be school caretakers. Don't look at us like that! Where else can you get paid for being stupid and shouting at kids all the time? (*Seriously, now, please. Caretakers are hard-working, skilled and dedicated people who spend all their time replacing light-bulbs and fixing toilets that obnoxious children break. They deserve medals! Teacher.*)

CDT

It is a fact that no one over the age of twenty-five has the faintest idea what CDT is – and that includes some of the teachers. (*Untrue! Every teacher knows it stands for Complete Dimbo Training. Teacher.*)

Our parents don't know what CDT stands for. In their day they did things like Woodwork and Technical Drawing and they think we still do it. When anyone asks what CDT is, we tell them whatever we feel like and they go storming off to school to ask what education is coming to these days and beat up the head teacher.

Here are a few suggestions you can try when faced with the ultra-boring question, 'What does CDT stand for?' You can probably think up better ones yourself!

> Canoe Dipping Techniques
> Canadian Duck Tracking
> Camel Dung Technology
> Cake Defrosting Techniques
> Certificate in Dangerous Terrorism
> Certificate in Drug Taking
> Chocolate Dessert Tasting
> Cat and Dog Theft
> Custard Doughnut Theory

Changing-rooms

If you're shy about showing your naughty bits in the changing-rooms, changing for games can be total hell. Our advice: never do games unless under the threat of death.

If you have to, buy yourself a pair of thick flesh-pink tights and a flesh-pink long-sleeved vest. Put these on, then put all your other clothes over the top. In the changing-room strip down to the tights and vest and slip into your games kit without showing a single centimetre of bare flesh. Brill, eh? And if anyone says anything about your skin being strange, say you've got *Knitvestia pinkia*, a nasty and extremely catching skin disease.

If you are a boy, wear a fur coat under your uniform. When you strip off your shirt and trousers, everyone will just think you are extremely hairy and grown up.

Also worth looking up COFFS AND COLDS and GAMES.

Coffs and Colds

We have coffs and colds all the time, except at weekends and during the holidays. They're not all real coffs and colds, of course. Sometimes we catch them by kissing people, other times we do a bit of acting! Coffs and colds are brilliant. If you wheeze enough, you can get out of games and singing. If you cough and sneeze enough, the teachers send you home cos they're scared they'll catch it too.

There's one other thing to mention about having a cold, and that's what to do with yeucky, snot-filled tissues. We dispose of them tidily, of course. We fold them up neatly and put them in other people's blazer pockets, football boots, pencil-cases and lunch-boxes. (*That's disgusting! Hold on a minute, my ham and banana sandwich tasted very*

27

strange and chewy this lunch-time. You didn't . . .?
Bleeeurgh! Teacher.)
Also worth looking up ACTING and BOGIES.

Computers

Have you noticed that most kids know a billion
times more about computers than the teachers who
are supposed to be teaching them? This is because
most teachers are so old they were born before
the invention of the microchip and they still have
problems with calculators, let alone your average
IBM PC. We keep Mr Bitty, our computer teacher,

under control by threatening to wipe his hard disk if he gives us any aggro.

Even if you don't know how to switch your school computer on, you can still have fun trying to crash the system. Just do as many daft things as you can. If, eventually, you manage to crash it, don't worry. There's always some kid, probably a weedy little first year with a brain the size of a double-decker bus, who can put it right again.

Concerts

We'd rather sit for a week in a bath full of school gravy than take part in a school concert, but if there's absolutely no escape, here's what to do:

• The orchestra. You can usually get out of the orchestra by playing really badly. If possible, choose to play an instrument you can't even hold properly. We find a violin is the best for making a truly terrible noise. When the music teacher chucks you out, don't forget to cry. If there's no escape, volunteer to play the drums and on the big night see if you can play louder than everyone else.

• The choir. If the music has different parts, always sing soprano. It's a giggle trying to hit the high notes, even if you don't get them. In fact, do your best to make sure you *never* hit the right note. On the big night, when you're standing there in rows like a load of stuffed possums, you can liven things up a bit by:

1. Trying to make everyone in your row fall over like a line of dominoes.

29

2. Yelling, 'Ahhhhh! A spider!'

3. Starting a Mexican wave.

If you play it right, next year you'll be banned from the concert altogether.

Corporal Punishment

Corporal Punishment is the leader of Sebastian's school cadet corps. All right, we'll tell the truth. Corporal punishment isn't allowed in schools these days, so if a teacher hits, prods or canes you, they're breaking the law; and although we don't take a lot of notice of most laws, this is one we're very fussy about. (*Gnash, gnash! It's not fair. I need some exercise for my slappy slipper! Teacher.*)

Also worth looking up CAPITAL PUNISHMENT.

Corridors

Hands up if you've ever been stopped for running in the corridors by teachers. Millions of you! But we've discovered that Sir Christopher Hen, who designed the first British school in 1066, had different ideas:

Ye corrydors are for ye pupils to run up and down in, forsooth, so they mayest test-drive their ultra-grip trainers when they go rounde ye corners. And verily, I thinkest it wouldst be a good ydea if they rode their bicycles in ye corrydors as well.

See? Brilliant, innit? So next time a teacher tells

you corridors aren't for running or riding your bike in, you just tell them Sir Christopher Hen said they were. (*There's something a bit fishy about all this . . . Teacher.*)

And if your teacher doesn't believe Sir Christopher Hen, you can always try another excuse. For example, whenever we get stopped we say that Miss Sprint from the PE department told us to run around more often. That usually stops them complaining long enough for us to run away!

Crazes

If you can't get into your bedroom cos it's full of ancient My Little Pony gear, or books of football stickers, or Turtle stuff, or 1,000 different pencil-cases or any other rubbish, you are a craze-aholic and you need expert help! And here it is.

What you should understand about most crazes is that they're invented by grown-ups to make money out of us kids. You mean you hadn't realized that, dopey? It's all a plot to make us kids spend our cash on things we don't really need. Grown-ups think we're stupid enough to spend our money on bits of useless plastic. Problem is, lots of kids *are*!

If you want to be cool, the last thing you should do is get involved in a craze. Crazes are for little kids. When did you last see your fave hero or heroine walking around in green furry Turtle slippers or showing off their collection of 749 pencil-rubbers?

Unless we start a craze ourselves, we don't get involved. Last year we started a craze for colouring our noses green with an eye-shadow pencil. Everyone at school copied us, so we stopped doing it. It took six weeks for them to realize the craze was over. Six weeks of them all walking around with green noses while we laughed ourselves silly!

Cricket

Cricket is a stupid game. What do you mean, you don't know the rules? They're easy! You're in until you're out. Then you go in until you're all out. Then you go out while the other team goes in and comes out one by one until they're all out and then you do it all over again, and days and days later everyone's out and everyone goes in and that's it. Gottit?

If you are ever forced to play this horrid game, pray for rain. If that doesn't work, here is some advice:

1. Never go anywhere near the ball. If you see it coming towards you, run away and hide.

2. If you have to bowl, aim to hit the batsperson on the head as hard as possible. (*I say, that isn't cricket! Teacher.*)

3. If you are given a bat, use it to knock the umpire over.

4. If you are fielding at the edge of the pitch, it's OK to lie down and have a snooze or a picnic lunch.

The best thing about cricket is the stupid terms given to the positions and the ways of bowling. For example, keep out of the way of *googlies* and aim for *silly mid-off*. Whoever invented cricket needs locking up if you ask us!

Also worth looking up BOOTS, CHANGING-ROOMS and GAMES.

Crisps

Crisps are just about the best invention ever. If it wasn't for them we'd starve to death. Always, always, ALWAYS take a bag of crisps with you wherever you go, even if it's only down the garden. You never know when you'll need them.

When you've eaten the crisps, the bag is very

useful. You can blow it up and bang it behind some incredibly old and nervous person and give them a nice surprise. (PS Don't blame us if the old person doesn't like it and dies.) Kylie's bedroom walls are covered in crisp packets, which give it a lovely cheese and oniony pong.

Our favourite flavour is hedgehog. We eat garlic flavour before French lessons, to get us into a pongy French mood. One of our favourite tricks is to put bacon crisps in a salt and vinegar packet and offer them to weedy vegetarians! One final bit of advice about crisps. Never eat ready-salted. They are poisonous to anyone under the age of twenty-one, which is why they're OK for grannies and old people, but not for you. (*Come off it, you two. Teacher.*)

Danger
School is a very dangerous place, so stay away from it if you can. Here are some dangerous things we've tried and DO NOT RECOMMEND.

1. Tasting the contents of all the bottles and jars in the chemistry lab.

2. Jumping out of the windows of any class-room above ground-floor level.

3. Throwing your rucksack over the top of the stairs. Sebastian got expelled for doing this at Harrough. His rucksack hit the headmaster on the head and knocked him out!

4. School lunches.

5. Going anywhere near the school gym.

6. Trying to catch a javelin.

Keep mentioning these dangers to your parents

or guardians until they get so scared something terrible will happen that they let you stay at home. **Also worth looking up DENTIST.**

Death
This is the last but most utterly brilliant way of really winding teachers up, because if you die on the school premises they have to fill in lots of horrible accident report forms and miss their coffee break, which makes them really, really angry. However, we DO NOT RECOMMEND dying at school. In fact we don't recommend dying at all, ever, if you can help it.
Also worth looking up DANGER.

Dentist

Going to the dentist is a good way of getting out of lessons. To be ultra-cool, you need to have a brace. We've both got braces on our top *and* bottom teeth, which means we hardly ever have to go to school cos we're always at the dentist having them adjusted. We also carry tiny screwdrivers around with us all the time, so we can undo our braces in emergencies and get rushed to the dentist to have them welded back on again.

HEALTH WARNING: Braces can be dangerous. We once tried to kiss each other and had to be cut apart by a fireman with a blowtorch. Not very romantic. Braces are also dangerous if brought into contact with school cabbage. If you try to eat cabbage while wearing a brace you will probably choke and die. So don't do it!

Also worth looking up DANGER, DEATH and DESPERATE MEASURES.

Desperate Measures

When you've done something totally terrible at school, you'll need desperate measures to get you out of trouble. If you have a passport and a lot of money, we suggest you leave the country. Australia or America are good places to escape to. If you are stuck, we advise you to confess what you've done before you are found out. Find the nicest teacher in the school (there must be *one* who's half-human!) and tell them. Teachers like this!

If you've got a test and can't do any of the questions, do a silent bottom burp and accuse someone else of doing it. While they're yelling, 'It wasn't me, sir!' and everyone else is racing for the windows, you can copy the answers off the brainy kid sitting next to you. Other ways of getting out of tests or serious trouble include crying, fainting, being sick and jumping out of windows.

Also worth looking up DANGER, DON'T KNOW and ENVIRONMENT.

Detention

Teachers hate detention because they have to stay late after school too, and they hate that cos they'll miss *Neighbours.* So remember that every time you get a detention you punish a teacher!

We try to get as many detentions as possible, which really winds the teachers up. In fact some of them punish us by *taking away* our detentions! If you don't want to get a detention, find out which days certain teachers *have* to leave school on time and wind them up on those days.

Dinner

Don't eat school dinner unless you are wearing protective clothing and have had your tonsils, taste-buds and tummy removed. Always check to make sure your burger is really dead. Never eat chips with a bit of black on them, or your hair will fall out. (*Nonsense! What's wrong with school dinners? I love them myself, all that lovely mashed swede and gooey custard full of chewy lumps, mmmmmm. Teacher.*)

Also worth looking up DANGER.

Dinner Ladies

Dinner ladies are all members of the strange and mysterious Burnemlumpi tribe, who come from the northern-most area of Birmingham. While they are just innocent girls their mothers teach them to cook the school kitchen way. They study until they can make pizzas so tough and crispy it's impossible to cut them with a hack-saw, and gravy so watery and full of strange lumps that not even the caretaker's cat can eat it. When they are fully trained they leave Birmingham and travel all over Britain to cook in schools and yell at kids.

If your dinner ladies can actually cook nice food, they are impostors and should be thrown out of the school meals service. There is a way of telling whether your dinner ladies are genuine Burnemlumpi tribe members or not. If you go up

to a real Burnemlumpi dinner lady and say, 'This
dinner is disgusting,' she will smile and say,
'Thank you.' If your dinner lady is an impostor,
she will hit you with a big spoon covered in apple
crumble. Try it and see what happens. (*Don't you
dare! Dinner ladies are angels and work hard
enough as it is. I love your food, ladies, I really
do! Teacher.*)
Also worth looking up DINNER.

Don't Know

'Don't know' is the safest thing you can say at
school. If you're a nervous person, don't say
anything else. It is also a very useful phrase if you
are pretending to have gone mad or lost your
memory. Here is an example of how it works:

Teacher: 'What is your name?'
You: 'Don't know.'
Teacher: 'Don't know what?'
You: 'Don't know.'
Teacher: 'Are you trying to wind me up?'
You: 'Don't know.'
Teacher: 'Would you prefer to eat a chocolate
    ice-cream or a cornet full of doggy-do?'
You: 'Don't know.'

And on, and on, and on, until one or other of
you goes totally bananas.

Dormitories

Dormitories are where you sleep in boarding-
school and they are usually great cos you can have
pillow-fights and midnight feasts. Sebastian has

two bits of advice if you are going to sleep in the dorm:

1. Do not wear your fluffy bunny pyjamas, or the pair with little pink flowers over them, if you are a boy.

2. Do not take Flopsy bunny, Mr Wibbly-Wobbly your clown doll or any other silly toy – no matter how much you love them. A teddy bear is OK, but wait till the other people in the dorm get theirs out first.

Also worth looking up BOARDING-SCHOOL.

Drama

We love drama classes! Yeahhh! They're the only time we can attack people in front of witnesses and get away with it. The secret of success in drama is staying in character. So if you 'accidentally' hit your best enemy in the drama

40

class, you can say, 'It wasn't me who hit him, miss, honest, it was my character.' Gottit?

The other thing we do in drama is brainwash the real dimmos. For example, one day Ms Panstick (the Bulldozer High drama teacher) asked us to imagine what would happen if a terrible plague broke out in the school and we all had to be locked in so that none of us passed the disease on to the rest of the world. By the end of the lesson Kylie had managed to convince one of the other kids that it had really happened. He was so scared that he gave her his dinner money in exchange for two 'magic' pills to cure him of the plague. And he didn't even notice they were Smarties!

Environment

'Environment' is a word which will come in useful for getting you out of trouble. The environment is everywhere·and everything, even things you can't see, like the holes in the bozo layer (*Ozone layer, idiots. Teacher.*) Here are some things that are ruining the environment and must be stopped:

1. Sebastian's smelly socks.
2. Cows.
3. Mr Moody the geografy teacher.

Even though it's dead boring, the environment is useful at school cos all the teachers except Mr Moody lie awake at night worrying about it. Whenever anything goes wrong they blame the environment. So when we get into trouble we blame it too. Brilliant, innit? Here are some examples:

Teacher: 'Why is your blazer full of holes?'
You: 'They're caused by acid rain and the environment.'
Teacher: 'Why are you late for school?'
You: 'I'm late because a rock fell off the moon and through a hole in the bozo layer and hit me on the head.'
Teacher: 'Why haven't you done the essay I set you?'
You: 'Because I ran out of environment-friendly recycled paper – and you wouldn't want me to use any other kind, would you?'

Escaping

Some kids are brilliant at escaping. One moment they're there, sitting at their desks, next second they've vanished. We should pay tribute to Clint 'the Shadow' Pennyfeather, whose vanishing tricks are so famous that the head teacher brought in Paul Daniels to explain how he did them – and Paul Daniels didn't know! Ha-ha! (*Sorry, Mr Daniels! The children are only joking. Teacher.*) That's what you think!

The best way of escaping is by running messages. So act as if you're a total goody-goody until the day a teacher asks you to take a message to someone. Deliver it and then escape. With a bit of luck, the teacher will forget all about you and you won't even be missed.

Sebastian's greatest escape was when he abseiled down the side of the science block. He'd learnt abseiling on a school trip – so always go on school trips, they may come in useful!

Essays

You don't actually *do* essays, do you? You do? Well, we don't! Here are some ways of getting out of trouble if you're supposed to have written an essay and you haven't.

Get a dog to eat it. This is easier if you have a Rottweiler than if you have one of those things like a poodle crossed with a hamster. It helps if you soak your 'essay' in meaty chunks first. Don't allow the dog to eat it all. When you've got just a few inches of paper left, grab it back and write a few words so it looks as if the rest have been eaten.

Write pages and pages in totally illegible gobbledegook, so it looks as if it just *might* be a brilliant essay. Your teacher will be too embarrassed to admit they can't read a single word of your writing and give you at least a C for writing so much.

Sabotage your school-bag. Rip a couple of teeth out of the zip of your school-bag, so the zip won't open more than an inch. When the teacher asks for your essay do a big, 'This is a terrible disaster! I can't get my essay out of my bag because the zip has stuck,' act. Teachers won't force the zip in case they break it and have to buy you a new bag. This trick is also useful for getting you out of PE – because, of course, your kit is stuck inside the bag. Isn't it?

Also worth looking up DESPERATE MEASURES.

Exam Results

If they're terrible, tell everyone that you failed your exams on purpose because you want to be incredibly rich and famous. Then point out that both Princess Diana and Prime Minister John Major were pretty unsuccessful at school. But look where they are now!

Also worth looking up DESPERATE MEASURES.

Exams

We've found the best way of coping with exams is not to do them. Kylie's favourite way for getting out of exams is to put ten packets of laxative in the staff-room tea urn. All the teachers are too busy queuing for the loo to worry about anything else. If you can't get out of exams by escaping or creating a diversion, like setting off the fire-alarm, and you are not a swot, you will have to cheat.

We've got electronic Psion organizers, which we programme with all the info and take into the exam room with us. If a teacher says anything, we tell them they're calculators! If you're a girl, you can write out the info on sheets of paper and put them down the inside of your tights just above the knee, so you can pull your skirt up and have a look. (A word of warning from Kylie, who found that this doesn't work if (a) you have a very short skirt and/or (b) you wear thick black woolly tights.)

Expulsion

Anybody can get themselves expelled from school. Look at the idiots and nutters who get chucked out of your school, for example. (*Look at Sebastian! Do you want to be like him? Kylie.*) The secret of being really cool and enjoying school is to stir things up just enough to make it exciting, but not so much that you get expelled. Teachers love it when kids get expelled because it saves them time and trouble. We don't want to give them that satisfaction, so we just bend their rules a bit, rather than break them. The only good reason for getting expelled is because you want to be – but remember, the next school might be even *worse* than the one you're at now!

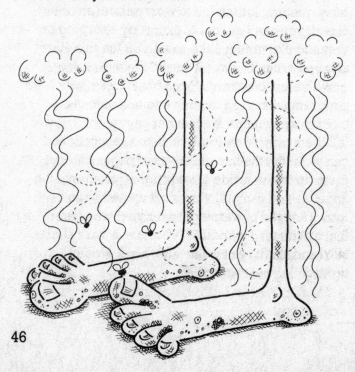

Feet

Never wash them and never, ever claim the odd
sock someone always finds at the end of PE
lessons. The people who claim odd socks either
have three legs, or they're seriously weird. Once
your feet are nicely smelly, you'll find that
teachers keep their distance and don't interfere
with what you're doing, which is great.
Also worth looking up ARMPITS.

Fire-drill

We like fire-drill, specially when it comes in the
middle of a double maths lesson. Have you noticed
that fire-drills only happen on nice sunny days?
That's because teachers don't like standing in
playgrounds in the rain, even though they make
us do it during wet break-times. You can have
some fun by hiding when the fire-bell goes, so
everyone has to look for you. Only hide if you're
sure it's not a real fire. It's not worth getting
burned just to avoid twenty minutes of maths – honest!

If you go to boarding-school you'll probably
have a fire-drill at night. You can have a good
giggle at the teachers in their Batman jim-jams and
fluffy nighties and curlers. The big problem about
night-time fire-drills is what you grab to take with
you when the bell goes. These are things you
should not take with you:

• Your school books. Let 'em burn!
• Anything pink and fluffy.
• Matches. These could be used as evidence
against you.

These are things you *should* take with you:
- Hair mousse, comb, hair-dryer, zit cream, make-up and jewellery.
- Your best trainers and other gear.
- Love-letters.

Foreign Teachers

Foreign teachers are easy prey! We have great fun teaching them all about the British way of life. For example, we taught Mademoiselle Seelee-Idyot that it was a quaint English custom to spit in the staff-room coffee-cups before serving coffee at break-time. And then we convinced Herr Hans Kneesandboompsidaisy that the word 'obnoxious' is used to describe something very nice. He went back to Germany after telling the headmaster what an obnoxious man he was. Ho-ho-ho. (*You two are so cruel . . . Tee-hee-hee. Teacher.*)

Forgery

Forgery comes in very useful for producing sick-notes. If possible, when you first start at school tell your teacher that no one in your family can write and so you'll have to write your own sick-notes and your parent or guardian will sign them. No, of course you don't actually *get* your parent or guardian to sign the notes, noddy! You do it all yourself. This means that you can have a day or a week off school whenever you feel like it.

If it's too late to claim that no one in your family can write, you could try pretending that your parent or guardian has broken their arm and can't

48

send a note. The last resort is forgery. Here are some forged sick-notes. You can copy them in your disguised handwriting and teachers will never know your mum didn't write them. (PS Remember to put your own name in instead of ours; it'll make all the difference.)

Dear Mrs Nikkery-Lastick,
Kylie wassnt at scool
yesterday becoz she had the
meesles.

With love from Kylie's mum.

Dear Mr Pimple,
Sebastian wasn't at school
yesterday because I asked him
to stay at home and polish the
Rolls-Royce.

Yours sincerely,
P. P. P. Spottly-Bott.

French
French is a very stupid language. For a start, it takes twice as long to say anything in French as it does in English, so you can only say half as much. And then there's the problem with words that sound the same and mean different things, like

mère meaning 'mother' and *mer* meaning 'sea', or *vert* meaning 'green' and *verre* meaning 'glass'. This causes a lot of problems when you try to say something like, 'The sea looks like glass,' which comes out sounding like, 'My mother looks green.'

Fortunately the Frenchies have realized how silly their language is and they are improving it by adopting lots of wonderful English words. So hooray for *le hot dog*, *le hamburger*, *le weekend*, *le chewing-gum* and *le car-park*. In ten years' time they'll all be speaking proper English like what we do, and we won't have to have no more French lessons.

Games

Games teachers say we have to do sport because it makes us big and strong and healthy. If that's true, why are people always injuring themselves playing football and Rugby and having heart attacks playing squash and running? And have you noticed that even Mr 'Incredible Hulk' Games Teacher always has a bad back? The truth is that Games is yet another way of making kids look and feel stupid. Why else would anyone make us stand around on a muddy field dressed in naff shorts or PE skirts, trying to knock a ball around? Nah – the only games we like are computer games!

Our advice is never to go near the gym or sports field, never to take off any clothing at school, and never to run unless you're in a school

corridor or there's a Rottweiler chasing you.
**Also worth looking up BOOTS, DANGER,
GAMES KIT and GAMES TEACHERS.**

Games Kit

With a bit of luck you'll never have to wear your
games kit. But even if you do, you must never
wash it. Only wimps and wallies wear washed and
ironed games kits. It takes about three years for
the average T-shirt and shorts to reach a perfectly
pongy condition. Ours are now at the stage where
they can stand up on their own, and Sebastian's
shorts are so full of microscopic wildlife that they
can slither across the changing-room floor on their
own.

These days, when we have to do sport, we find we're never picked for any of the teams and when we play hockey or netball or football, no one comes near us or sends the ball in our direction. Great, innit? Kylie once played a hockey match all on her own. She just walked on the pitch and the other team ran off holding their noses. She won the game 317–0! **Also worth looking up ARMPITS, BOOTS, GAMES and HALITOSIS.**

Games Teachers

Most PE teachers have less intelligence than the average slug – otherwise they wouldn't be PE teachers, would they? When students enrol at PE college anyone who is intelligent, charming, kind or even just half-way human is weeded out so that only the most horrible get to work in our schools. The way to wind PE teachers up is to be very intelligent and remind them that they're not. Say these things in front of them and see what happens:

• 'The *Financial Times* had an article this morning showing that if you do more than three minutes' exercise a day, your brain turns to jelly.'

OR

• 'Did you know that the Arabs have around 1,000 different words for "camel"?'

OR

• 'Did you know that they make so much chocolate in Switzerland that every person living there could eat two large bars a day – and there'd still be some left over?'

Warning: Do not make your PE teachers too angry. Some of them are ex-army instructors trained to shoot on sight and kill people with one twist of their little fingers, so be careful!

(PE teachers are wonderful people. It's not their fault they're a bit dim, is it? Teacher. Aaaaagh! Stop hitting me with that hockey stick, Miss Sprint!)

Also worth looking up DANGER and GAMES.

Genius

There are only three geniuses (*Shouldn't that be genii? Teacher.*) in the world. There's the two of us and there's you, too. We don't care what everyone says, you're a genius – you must be for choosing this book!

Geografy

Geografy is the most boring subject in the entire universe. Before they are allowed to teach it, geografy teachers have to make a promise that they will never tell us kids anything useful or interesting about the world. This is why we have to learn about rocks and glaciers and all that rubbish, when what we really want to know is which countries are the best for holidays. These are the things geografy should really be about:

- Beaches and swimming pools – which countries have the best?
- Theme parks and things to do – which countries have the most?
- Food – which countries have chips and Coke?

What else does anyone need to know about the world? Nothing!

Ghosts

All schools are haunted by the ghosts of the kids and teachers who died of boredom during double physics and double maths. You don't believe us? Ask your head teacher if he or she believes in such a thing as the school spirit. Bet you a billion zillion trillion Mars Bars they say yes!

Seeing a ghost can be a useful way of getting out of trouble. Next time you're seriously late, walk into the class-room looking all white and scared and say you saw a ghost gliding along the corridor. That should distract the teacher from yelling at you for a bit.

Also worth looking up DESPERATE MEASURES.

Gossip

We think you should be able to get GCSEs in gossip. Just think about it. To be good gossips we have to use our imagination, our communication skills and our maths to add two and two together and make five. It's hard work, and we deserve a grade A for it!

Anyone can pass gossip on, but it takes true geniuses, like us, to start it off. The more outrageous the stories you tell about other people, the better. If you see spotty Damien from down the road out with a girl, it's no good telling everyone *that*. That's news, not gossip. No, for real gossip you have to say that you saw him kissing a girl who appears on telly in *Grange Hill* when he was supposed to be out with his girlfriend, and they were both arrested by a policeman. It'll be around the school in no time and you'll know it's all because of *you*! Yeahhh!

Gravy

School gravy is useful stuff, but it has to be handled carefully. For example, it can burn its way through wood and plastic, so if you want to carry it around with you you'll have to use a glass or metal bottle. You can use it to drill holes in wooden desks. Just put a drop on the top of the desk and stand back. We reckon six pints of gravy should be enough to dissolve a class-room full of furniture.

Gravy is also the world's best glue, but there is no known way of unsticking it. If there is someone you really hate, put gravy on the loo seat. They will have to spend the rest of their lives sitting there!

If you mix two spoons of school gravy with one spoon of rice pudding and a pinch of dandruff, you get the most powerful explosive in the world. So be very, very careful next time there's gravy and rice pudding on the menu at school and don't shake your head over the plate. Otherwise there might be a huge bang and the entire school will disappear in a puff of smoke.

Also worth looking up DANGER and DINNER.

Gum

We always keep a few bits of ready-chewed gum

handy, stuck behind our ears. It's good for sticking
notices to the wall if you run out of Blu-tack, and
for sticking the pages of your workbook together
so that teachers can't read the essays you didn't
write. If you bung a bit of chewing-gum on your
knife at lunch-time, you can pick up peas more
easily. When we've finished lunch, we stick the
plates together with gum, too. It keeps the dinner
ladies busy.

PS **Health warning:** Don't leave ready-chewed
gum behind your ears for too long. Sebastian did,
and had to have his ears surgically removed in
hospital.

Haircuts

Forget your flat-top and Mohican, our theory is that there are only four basic types of haircut – the Pudding Basin, the Hedgehog, the Mr Whippy and the Baldie. We like the Hedgehog best because the others are neat and tidy and we are *never* neat and tidy.

We never have our hair cut during term-time. If it *has* to be cut, we get it done during the holidays so it has a week or two to grow again before we go back to school. This saves everyone the terrible shock of seeing our ears. We used to go to Vidal Sassoon and have our hair trimmed, but they never got the style quite right. These days we cut each other's hair using a kitchen knife or by lying down in front of the lawn-mower in the park. It's cheaper and the results are far better.

If you want to dye your hair a new colour, we have a handy hint. The teachers will go berserk if you turn up with bright-blue or purple hair, so we suggest you choose the colour of your school uniform. This way it blends in better and they can't complain so much!

Halitosis

Halitosis is the posh way of saying 'bad breath'. We're really proud of ourselves, because our breath is so disgusting we can knock over first years standing 100 metres away!

How can you get to this peak of pongy perfection? All you have to do is stop brushing your teeth and eat six cloves of garlic, two onions

and a packet of salt and vinegar crisps after each meal. Once you've got bad breath, you're safe at school. Bullies don't come near you, just in case you open your mouth, and teachers keep a safe distance away and don't give you too much hassle. So go on, chuck those tooth-brushes away and start building up a lovely furry yellow coating on your tongue!

Also worth looking up ARMPITS and FEET.

Hamsters
We believe it's really cruel to keep hamsters locked up in cages at school, with kids poking and squeezing them all day, so we have formed the Hamster Liberation Front, which aims to set all school hamsters (and gerbils) free. So far we have liberated nineteen hamsters and four gerbils, and

they are all living happily together in Sebastian's wardrobe at home. When we last checked there were 1,683 of them, but they were breeding faster than we could count. The man at the pet shop gives us 10p per hamster, so we should be millionaires by 1995! If you want to join the Hamster Liberation Front, send £500 to: HLF, Rodent House, Mousehole, Cornwall, and we will send you a hamster liberation kit and information about how to stop people hamster-hunting and wearing hamster-fur coats.

Head Teachers
No one in their right mind would want to be a head teacher, so only mad people apply for the job. Remember, their job puts them under a lot of strain, and if you're not careful they may go totally bananas and do strange things like expelling you for no reason at all. So always be gentle with the head teacher. When you meet them, stroke their hands and say, 'Feeling a bit better today, are we?' This is everything you need to know about head teachers.

History
History is a sexist subject. Why isn't it called herstory? Or theirstory? This is a brilliant reason for refusing to go to history lessons. At Kylie's school all the girls refused to do history because it was just about kings and armies and men, and there was nothing about women in it. We mean, all the women must have been doing interesting things while the men were off fighting boring wars, mustn't they? So if you really want to get out of doing

history, bring up this subject and keep complaining about it. Eventually, just to get some peace, the teacher will let you go and do something else. **Also worth looking up ISMS.**

Holidays
Holidays are great, aren't they? And what makes holidays so awesomely wonderful? School – cos if we didn't have to go to school, we'd have holidays all the time and then they'd get boring. You might actually find yourself wanting to go to school! Strange, innit, but it makes sense. So when you're really sick of school, just remember. The worse you feel about going, the better the holidays are. Just think of all those swots who love school. They must really hate the holidays!

The other thing about holidays is that if you go away somewhere, you must never go where everyone else has been, cos you want to be a bit different, don't you? So if they've all been to Spain or Greece, you tell 'em you've been somewhere really exotic. You don't have to go, of course. You just look in an atlas and find somewhere that sounds really good. Last summer we went to Omsk. Next year we're thinking of going to Plovdiv or Pljevlja. No idea where they are, but they sound right good, don't they?

Idiots
You can always spot an idiot by what they carry. If anyone you know possesses any three of these items, you can tell them they're an official idiot:

- Glasses held together with Elastoplast.
- A can of Tizer.
- Gloves threaded through their sleeves on a bit of elastic.
- Fish-paste sarnies.
- Completed chemistry homework.
- A train-spotter's handbook.
- An odd sock.
- An anorak.

(I'm sure I took the Elastoplast off my glasses last week. And anoraks are very comfortable, so don't go knocking them. Has anyone seen my fish-paste

sandwiches, by the way? Teacher.) If you turn out to be an idiot, then please shut this book now and give it to someone else. We didn't write it for people like *you* to read.

Inglish

Sebastian's Inglish teacher is Mr Pratt. We call him Total and the best way of winding him up is to spell things wrong. So though we can spell brilliantly, in Inglish we make lots of mistakes and send him crazy.

Wun of the fings we liik abowt Inglish is ritin powetri. Here is a powem wot we rote:

> I luv to do my howmwerk,
> It mayks mee fiel so good.
> I luv to do evryfing
> Teecher says I shud.
> I luv to do my essays,
> I do them evry day.
> Hoo are these men in wite coats
> Hoo are tayking me away?

Invisibility

Have you noticed that some kids at school are almost invisible? In every class there's always one kid you hardly ever notice, isn't there? In fact, no one takes any notice of them at all. This is great if you want to get up to things, because no one notices what you're doing.

We'd like to be invisible, but we look too wicked and we've got too much to say for

63

ourselves. But if our kind of anarchy isn't your style, you can have a lot of fun by being invisible. To be invisible you have to try and look incredibly ordinary, so you're always getting mistaken for other people. You also have to be really quiet, so no one knows what you think.

There's another way of becoming invisible, or so we've been told. But as you have to eat six worms, stand on your head for two days and dance in a circle singing, 'Hiccuppy-lickuppy transit van/ Turn me into the invisible man,' we haven't tried it. And we suggest you don't bother, either.

Isms

Isms are useful if you want to cause a bit of excitement at school. For example, if a teacher says to you, 'I can hardly see you behind that desk, shortie,' you can have a big row about heightism and get them into trouble. Other good isms are sexism, ageism and racism. You can always start a good argument in the class-room by accusing someone of racist or sexist remarks.

We've also got a new ism: alphabetism. Alphabetism is all about discrimination because of the first letter of your surname. If your surname is Adams or Bennett, you're always at the top of the register and any other list that's organized by the alphabet. If you're called Young or Zilch, you have to wait around for your name to be called, and when reports or results are being given out, you're the last to get them. This is not fair! We are

64

determined to stamp out alphabetism at school, so we swap our surnames every day, which allows people to have a turn at the top of the register, and keeps the teachers confused. Why not give it a go and see what happens? (*No, don't do it! I'd have to spend all day rewriting the register. There'd be no time for lessons! Teacher.*)

Jabs

School nurses use blunt needles so that when they give you a jab it really, really hurts, and your arm swells up like a balloon and drops off. And the nurse is coming round to give everyone mega-injections next Monday. Didn't you know? Aaaaaaagh!

Ha-ha! That made you go all weak and wobbly, didn't it? But it's all right, you can stop crying now because we were only joking. We love having jabs, because it gets us off lessons and it really doesn't hurt much. Next time the nurse comes round with that syringe, be brave. There's nothing to get worked up about. It's just a sharp needle being stuck into your arm, innit? . . . Why have you gone so white all of a sudden?

Also worth looking up DANGER and NURSE.

Jam

We always carry a pot of raspberry jam in our rucksacks because it comes in very useful. If you get in a fight or want to look as if you've had an accident, you just smear a bit on your face and everyone thinks you're bleeding and you get taken to the sick-bay. If you're in the hockey or football or anything-else team and you have to

shake hands with your opponents, it's nice to have a big blob of jam in your palm. The other team get all sticky and won't play so well!

We also use it to play tricks in chemistry lessons. When we have to mix chemicals and see what they produce, we bung a blob of jam in a clean test-tube. The teacher comes around saying, 'And what did you get when you put hydrochloric acid into sulphate of ammonia?' We whip out the test-tube and say, 'Raspberry jam,' which always gets them excited. If you don't like jam you could always use peanut butter instead.

PS Don't use peanut butter for fake blood. It's not the right colour, for a start, and since when has your blood been full of crunchy bits?

Also worth looking up DESPERATE MEASURES.

Jewellery

Teachers hate jewellery because it's sparkly and fun and then don't earn enough money to buy any. Kylie wears two necklaces, three pairs of ear-rings, dozens of jangly bracelets and about twenty rings. Sebastian doesn't wear quite so many bracelets. Teachers say they don't want us wearing jewellery because it's dangerous, but how many people do you know who've been injured by a bangle? And if it's so dangerous, how come teachers wear it too? We think all kids should wear jewellery, and that way the teachers will be so busy telling everyone to take it off that they'll never get any lessons done!

Jobs

Have you ever wondered why you have to go to boring school now? Bad news. It's so you can get a boring job later! For a long time we thought that once we'd finished school life would be just awesomely amazing. Then we realized that after school comes something even worse. Jobs.

Parents and teachers will tell you to become an accountant or a bank manager or a solicitor or a librarian or something that only crumbly old people enjoy doing. They never suggest you become a professional sky-diver, or an explorer, or a chocolate-biscuit taster or a fryer in a chip shop, because they think those aren't good jobs. The secret of surviving is to tell all old people that you want to be something really serious like a brain surgeon, and just tell your friends that you're going to be a film star. That way you keep everyone happy.

As for us, we haven't made up our minds what we want to be. Maybe we'll be dentists and give people incredibly painful fillings. Maybe we'll be bus drivers and refuse to stop when people ring the bell. Whatever we do, we'll never be boring!

Jumble Sales

We've found a brilliant way to raise money at the school jumble sale. When teacher tells us to bring in old jumble, we and our friends bring along our family's favourite possessions. Sebastian brings in his dad's golf-clubs and his mum's best sparkly ball-gown. Kylie brings in her mum's signed

picture of Barry Manilow and her dad's black
leather motor-bike jacket.

A few days before the jumble sale our parents
suddenly notice that their golf-clubs, jackets, etc.
are missing and then we do a bit of innocent acting
and say, 'Oh, I took it down to the school jumble
sale.' Our parents then go whizzing off to school
and have to give the head teacher loadsamoney
to get their things back. Brill, innit?

Kissing

Most kids spend a lot of their time thinking about
kissing. Well we do! There's no big secret about
kissing. You just put your lips together and wiggle
about a bit and that's it. The most difficult thing is
finding the right person to kiss. If you've read our
advice on ARMPITS, FEET and HALITOSIS you'll
understand why you need to be careful. Here are
some people and things it is not a good idea to
kiss:

- The school caretaker's Rottweiler.
- The Queen.
- Frogs (you never know, you might end up with a
boring prince with sticking-out ears).
- Anything covered in Super-glue.
- Feet.
- Policemen (specially if you are a boy).
- Anyone else's girlfriend/boyfriend.
- Do not try to kiss your teacher, no matter how
much you like them – you weird kid!

Lavatories/Toilets

Toilets make great hang-outs if you've bunked off a lesson, but they're even better places to play tricks. Our favourite toilet trick is to lift up the loo seat, cover the bowl with cling-film and then put the seat back down again. Then hang about outside the cubicles and wait for the screams!

The other way of driving teachers and caretakers crazy is to get the thinnest or most acrobatic person in your class to go into the cubicle, lock the door and then either slide out under the 2-inch gap under the door, or climb over into the next cubicle. When they're all locked from the inside, run like mad!

Laws

There are two sets of laws in most schools. There are the teachers' laws, which are all those boring rules like no running and no make-up and no chewing-gum and all that. And then there are our laws, which the teachers don't know anything about. Our laws include:

1. Always slam doors as hard as you can.
2. Always leave a skateboard at the top of the stairs.
3. Always run, never walk – unless the teacher tells you to run, in which case, walk.
4. Leave something you need at home every day. (Not your lunch, stupid!)
5. Always shout in the library.
6. Never drop crisp packets and litter on the floor, but hide it wherever you can!

That's just a few of the kid's laws. If you obey them, you'll soon drive the teachers totally insane! (*Why do you keep slamming that door, Sebastian? And what's this skateboard doing – aaaaaaghh! Teacher.*)

Lost Property

Somewhere in your school, probably in the secretary's office, there is a cupboard marked Lost Property. It's full of horrible things, like 2,000-year-old gym shorts, matchboxes full of dead beetles, a million smelly odd socks that no one has ever claimed, footballs with punctures, handkerchiefs with all kinds of disgusting things in them, worms and bicycle-pumps that don't work.

The mysterious thing about this cupboard is you'll never find anything you lose in it. Nice things, like your high-top trainers, your pen that writes with gold ink, your potato pellet gun or your *Die Hard 2* video never, ever end up in the lost property cupboard. Neither does your lost maths homework or your CDT project work. Where do they go? No one knows, not even the police. This is a scandal and something should be done about it. We've written to our MP at the House of Commons and asked him to look into the lost property cupboard mystery. Why don't you do the same thing. Just send your letter to: Boring

Old MPs, House of Commons, London, England, Europe, the World, the Universe . . .

Lunch-boxes
We've invented this theory called the Lunch-box Theory. We've discovered that we can tell all about a person by taking a look at their lunch-box and the things in it. Check this list and see what your lunch-box says about you:

Lunch-boxes:
● Teddy Ruxpin lunch-box: you're a total and utter wally.
● Postman Pat lunch-box: you're a wimpy first year.
● Thomas the Tank Engine lunch-box: you're a train-spotting idiot.
● Tesco/Sainsbury carrier-bag: you're dead boring.

Contents:
● Marmite and muesli wholemeal sandwiches: you are a vegetarian.
● Fish-paste sarnies: you're an idiot.
● Tuna fish, marmalade and Brylcreem sandwiches: either you're really hard or your mum made your sandwiches with her eyes closed.
● No lunch-box, no lunch: wow, a real cool dude. Put it there!

And now a word of advice for anyone who gets their lunch nicked. If you want to stop it happening, you've got to think up some unusual sandwiches which no one will want to swipe. Try octopus and custard, beetroot and Vaseline or Fairy Liquid and rhubarb. We promise no one will eat your sandwiches. Trouble is, neither will you. **Also worth looking up CRISPS.**

Lying

The most important thing you learn at school is how to lie. Everyone does it all the time. Well, *we* do. If you can tell a lie without crying, going red or making your nose grow an inch, you can get away with almost anything.

But sometimes we actually tell the truth! Yeah, it's incredible, innit? We're not lying. Though they look like a load of old hippies, some teachers are intelligent enough to work out that we tell lots of porky-pies. So every now and then we tell the truth, which really gets them confused. Here's how it goes.

Teacher: 'Did you break that window?'

Kylie (truthfully): 'Yes.'

Teacher: 'I don't believe you. You're always telling lies. It must be someone else. Nigel Kipper, was it you?'

Nigel (truthfully): 'No, miss.'

Teacher: 'Aha! It's no good lying to me! I know it was you.'

Fools them every time!

Also worth looking up ACTING.

Make-up

Do you know why teachers hate kids wearing

make-up? It's because make-up makes us look incredibly beautiful and reminds them how incredibly old and wrinkly they are. That's why they try to stop us wearing it.

Some kids wear a teensy-weensy bit of make-up and hope the teachers don't spot it and make them rub it off. But what's the point of wearing make-up if no one knows you've got it on? If you're going to wear make-up you've got to wear lots and lots of it – that's what we think. So last term we went into school every day wearing orange eye-shadow and shiny green lipstick. By the end of term the teachers were so sick of telling us to take it off they agreed that everyone could have a bit of ordinary make-up. So everyone at our school wears blue eye-shadow and a splodge of mascara and lots of lovely red lipstick and looks awesomely gorgeous – even the lads!

Also worth looking up JEWELLERY.

Maths

Aaaaaaaaaaargh! Eeeeeeeeeeeeeeeeeek! Maths is mega-boring. No, we're wrong, it's even worse than that. Every day millions of innocent children are tortured by being made to do maths lessons and someone should stop it. We think the Queen should pass a law against it and lock up all the maths teachers in the Tower of London.

Meat

Have you ever noticed that the meat they serve for school dinners doesn't look or taste anything like the meat you get at home? It's not like beef or lamb or pork or chicken, is it? No. And we know why. We've been snooping and have discovered that the meat they serve in schools is none other than Moronosaurus meat! Unbelievable, but true!

The Moronosaurus is a kind of dinosaur which experts thought had died out about a billion years ago. It is 60 metres long, 14 metres high and has a brain even smaller than the most stupid person in your class. But though everyone thought the Moronosaurus was extinct, it's in fact alive and well and being bred on a top-secret farm near Lower Bumthorpe. It's such a huge animal that just one Moronosaurus produces enough meat to feed a million school-kids. So now you know the terrible truth. Next time your mum asks what you had for dinner at school today, don't say 'Beef curry', say 'Moronosaurus curry.' (*Are you absolutely sure about this, you two? Teacher.*)
Also worth looking up DINNER and DINNER LADIES.

Mistakes
Everyone makes mistakes in their schoolwork, even us. In fact some of our mistakes are even better than the things we get right. Here are a few of our favourite errors!
- The Sewage Canal is in Egypt.
- An executive is a person who cuts people's heads off.
- An oxygen has eight sides.

76

- The little worms you find in apples are called magnets.
- The ladies who serve dinner on aeroplanes are called hostages.
- People who live in Paris are called Parisites.
- My dog has had a litre of puppies.
- When you talk to people you have a conservation.

What was that? You can't see any mistakes? You are *really* stupid, aren't you?

Museums

You probably think museums are really boring places. But you're wrong! The problem is, most people don't know what to do when they go to museums. They tiptoe around and whisper, which is not the way to behave. Here are some things you should do.

Do the echo test. Some museums are huge places with high ceilings. We always yell or sing a song to see if there's an echo. Always do this if there's a sign saying 'Quiet Please', because it's usually a guarantee that there's a brilliant echo.

Scream incredibly loudly every time you see something scary, like an Egyptian mummy or a horrible statue. Natural history museums are full of lovely bugs and spiders that can keep you screaming for hours.

Play on the dinosaurs. Dinosaur skeletons make ace climbing-frames, and if you get to the top there's nothing the museum attendant can do to get you down!

Move signs. Some museums are asking for trouble because they don't nail their information signs to the walls. We like to move them around a bit. We once swapped the signs for a stuffed gorilla and for a portrait of Queen Victoria. Everyone stood in front of the gorilla and read 'Queen Victoria at the age of forty', and when they got to the portrait it said 'Rare example of mountain gorilla'. And you know what? Most of the people didn't realize anything was wrong!

Also worth looking up ART GALLERIES.

Names

Some names are wicked – like Sebastian and Kylie, for example. Whayyyy! But some names are mega-embarrassing when the teacher calls them out on the register. If you're called something weird like Alfred or Guinevere, or just something boring like Michael or Emily, you need to change your name quick! Sebastian used to be called Leonard Aubrey Spottley-Bott until he became Sebastian Sunshine Scott Spottly-Bott. Much better, innit? Here are a few you could choose from, depending on what image you want to create:

Brill names	Nerdy names	Old Fogey names
Sebastian	Nigel	Doris
Kylie	Morris	Albert
Marty	Ivanhoe	Fred
Charlene	Humphrey	Sidney
Michelangelo	Roland	George
Jason	Kevin	Dobbin
Green	Reggie	Rex
Ryan	Errol	Crystal
Trudy	Henrietta	Humphrey
Donatello	Flora	Angela
Marlene	Margarine	Ermintrude
Madonna	Mary	Jocasta
Scott	Saddam	Dick
Darlene	Maxwell House	Harold
Garth	Blackadder	Patience
Clint	Baldrick	Impatience
Humphrey	Tesco	In-Patients

Here's a space for you to write in your totally wicked new name:

Marty Charlene Scott

Nicking

Nicking goes on all the time at school, so you'd better watch out for your things. If you don't take anything to school you won't get anything stolen – but as it's not a good idea to go to school in the nude, you will have to take some anti-theft precautions. Here are our suggestions:

- Lunch-boxes: protect your sandwiches by putting a mousetrap in the box. If that's not enough, try a small but extremely poisonous snake.
- Rucksacks: a small alligator fits into a rucksack nicely and will stop people borrowing your things when your back is turned – though watch out they don't steal the alligator. If the alligator *does* go missing, you will be able to identify the thief by the teeth marks all over them. Watch out for severed hands cluttering up your rucksack too!
- Brief-cases: brief-cases make good homes for tarantula spiders, which are big and hairy enough to scare most people off. If you go to a really hard school you may have to resort to a scorpion with a deadly sting. For safety's sake, stick a notice saying 'Danger, deadly scorpion patrol' on the outside of the brief-case. Then if anybody gets killed, it's their own fault.
- Trainers: Super-glue your trainers to your feet so that no one can get them. You can also try welding the laces together.
- Walkman: we heard of a total dimmo who kept his Walkman safe by nailing the earphones to his head, but we DO NOT RECOMMEND you to do

this. Fortunately this stupid person had a brain so small that the nails missed it, but you might not be so thick. We keep our Walkmans in our spider-patrolled brief-cases when we're not actually using them.

● Jackets: we always get our jackets and coats from Oxfam, so it doesn't matter if they get stolen. If you've got an expensive jacket that's worth nicking, we suggest you customize it so that everyone knows it's yours. You could write your name across the back of a leather jacket with

studs, or sew a badge or patch on. Or put an electric-shock alarm in the pocket, so the second someone puts their hand in they light up like an electric lamp.

● Money: we never carry cash, but our poodles Fang and Snappy do. They come to school with us and carry our money in black leather purses attached to their collars – and (surprise, surprise), we've never been robbed yet!

If you can't afford an alligator, a spider or a scorpion, don't worry. Just tell everyone you've got one and pretend to be very careful each time you open your lunch-box or rucksack. Nobody will be sure whether it's true or not, but they won't take the risk of finding out.

Nicknames

Nicknames are OK if you've got a nice nickname, like Supercool or Wild Child, but what if you're known as Spotty or Space Cadet or Head Case? Not quite so good, is it? If you suspect you're about to get a horrible nickname, the best thing to do is make up your own good one and get your friends to call you that. Soon everyone else will pick it up too. The best nicknames relate to the way you look or behave. Choose something you like about yourself and turn it into a nickname. Be realistic when you're choosing your name. If you're thin and weedy, don't call yourself Rocky or Rambo unless you really want everyone to laugh.

Also worth looking up NAMES.

Nits

Nits like to live in clean hair, so we never wash ours in case we catch them. We use this fact to taunt any squeaky-clean kids who get at us for being grubby. They're the ones most likely to have nits, not us!

Anyway, what's everyone got against nits? We feel sorry for them. In fact we're so concerned that we're thinking of turning our heads into nit conservation areas so that nits never become extinct. If you'd like to save wildlife, you could do the same.

Also worth looking up ARMPITS, FEET and HALITOSIS.

Nudity

Nudity is not a good idea at school. Imagine the

problems you might have in the chemistry lab if you dripped some acid. Or in home economics if you were frying chips. Or in the workshop. Ouch! No, it's definitely a good idea to keep all your clothes on at school.

The only place you can safely take your clothes off is in the showers after PE. And as you'd have to be mad to want to take your clothes off in front of everyone else and stand under a cold shower, we suggest you don't do it. If the teacher insists, do what we do: go in with all your clothes on and then get sent home to change. This is a specially brilliant idea if you've got some horrible lesson like maths after PE!

Also worth looking up CHANGING-ROOMS and DESPERATE MEASURES.

Nurse

The school nurse or medical officer is a good person to go to – if you've got nothing seriously wrong with you. Every time we go to the school nurse (which, funnily enough, is always before French and physics lessons) she just makes us lie down for five minutes or gives us an aspirin or a mint to suck. Now this is OK if you've only got a headache or you're acting, but what if you're *really* ill? We mean, it's no good going to the nurse with appendicitis and being given a mint to suck, is it? You might die!

We never go to the nurse when we've got little cuts or grazes because she, and all the other school medical officers, have been trained to put undiluted TCP on them, which is agony and far worse than just running around with a grazed knee.

Oranges

Oranges are good for you, but don't worry – we're not going to tell you to eat them. No, if our mums give us oranges we use them for brilliant weapons. If you take a nice juicy orange, make a hole in it with a pencil and then squeeze, you can use it as a juice gun. Just aim a quick squirt of juice between your enemy's eyes and watch them run! And when you're out of juice you can kick the orange around the playground instead of a football. Much better than having to eat it, eh? **Also worth looking up BANANAS.**

Outings

There are some school outings you should go on and some school outings you should avoid like the plague. Stay away from anything that teachers call 'educational', because educational's just a long word for 'boring'. If there are any school outings the teachers moan about, sign up immediately because it means they'll be dead good. Here are some places to go to:

> Alton Towers
> Chessington World of Adventure
> Alton Towers
> London Zoo
> Blackpool
> Alton Towers

Here are some outings *not* to go on:

> A trip to the local sewage farm.
> Any building that has fallen down (unless there's a theme park nearby).
> A visit to a nature reserve.
> Any museum with old bits of pottery and rubbish in it.
> Visits to the theatre (specially if there's a boring old play by mega-boring William Shakespeare on).
> A stately home (except Alton Towers).

Also worth looking up ART GALLERIES and MUSEUMS.

Oxford

Oxford's a nice place. It's got lots of good shops and things to do. The only bad thing about Oxford is a load of boring old buildings filled with tourists taking pictures. These old buildings are bits of Oxford University, which is dead famous. That's why you may have heard your parents and teachers talk about sending you there.

The bad news is that to go to Oxford University you need about 200 grade 'A' GCSEs, which is why grown-ups are always nagging you to work harder. You also need to ride a bicycle and be brilliant at rowing, because every year all the students at Oxford University get in a boat and row down the River Thames and beat the students from Cambridge in the Boat Race.

Unless you're incredibly brainy and can swim (in case you fall out of the boat and into the river) we don't recommend you go to Oxford.
Also worth looking up UNIVERSITY.

Pens

It's seriously uncool to carry a pen or pencil around with you at school. If you do, teachers might expect you to write or draw something and you don't want to have to do that, do you? Not having a pen or pencil is a brilliant way of wasting at least the first five minutes of almost every lesson. If you've also forgotten your homework, your workbook and everything else you need, you can disrupt the whole lesson and drive the teacher really crazy!

The other thing about pens is that they're always disappearing. Have you noticed that? We did some research and reckon that on average at least 100 million pens get lost each year. But where do they all go? That's what we'd like to know. We've looked everywhere, including the lost property cupboard, but we can't find them. There are two possible explanations:

1. They are stolen by school dinner-ladies and melted down to make gravy.

2. There is a giant black hole in outer space that is gradually sucking all the pens off this planet.

Please let us know immediately if you have a different explanation.

Pets
AMAZING FACT: did you know that if you spell PETS backwards you get STEP? Incredible, innit? (*And did you know that if you spell SCHOOL backwards you get LOOHCS? Teacher.*)

Pets like going to school. Kylie's dog used to go to school with her every day, but he doesn't any more. He passed his exams and now he's at sixth-form college in Barking! Cats like school and so do guinea-pigs and rabbits. However, hamsters are short-sighted and cannot see the blackboard, so they never learn much.

School is a dangerous place for any animal smaller than a mouse. Eric, Sebastian's pet earwig, was accidentally trodden on during a game of Rugby just as he was about to pass the ball. And a friend of ours, Morris Minor, was very upset when he took his pet chicken to school, left it in the playground and later ate it with sage and onion stuffing for lunch. Those dinner ladies will cook anything!

Big pets can cause problems too. Did you read in the paper that a whole class of third-years were crushed by a badly-behaved elephant at Tickleham School? Apparently the elephant got angry when the teacher made a mistake and only gave it C+ for history. Elephants are brilliant at history; they always get As!

(*Short-sighted hamsters? Elephants doing history? Don't believe a word of it. Aaaaagh! What's that camel doing in my class-room? Teacher.*)

Physics

Physics lessons are good places to get your revenge on your worst enemies. When you're doing experiments with electricity, it's quite easy to wire someone up to the battery – accidentally, of course – and give them a bit of a shock! It's also easy to scorch them a bit with a Bunsen burner. Be careful, though. We're not talking serious injuries here, and we won't come and visit you in prison if you get arrested.

We were hoping that the GCSE course would include details of how to make bombs, which would be incredibly useful. Bad news though – you don't do bombs till A level. (*Phew, what a relief! Teacher.*)

Poetry

In the old days poetry was very difficult because it had to rhyme and all the lines had to be the same length and start with capital letters. School kids had a hard time trying to find rhyming words for 'orange' and 'potato'. These days poetry is really easy. You just write down anything you like and it's a poem. To prove it, here is one of Kylie's love poems:

> I wish I was
> A ten ton squirrel
> Sitting in a tree,
> And when you passed below my branch
> I'd drop on you and squash you
> Flat.

Here are some lines for you to write your own poem:

I'd wish my love woz a red rose
With lots of prickles on the stem
I'd ask you to pick it for me
& cut your ~~st~~ wrist and
BLEED TO DEATH!

Amazing! A really brilliant poem!

Pop Music

Teachers don't understand that kids today just have to have music all the time. In their day all

91

they had were huge gramophones and crackly old records of opera singers and hippie bands like the Rolling Stones. And who'd want to listen to *them*? No wonder teachers hate music.

If we want to wind teacher up we don't play music in the class-room, cos that way our tapes just get confiscated. We sit in class with our Walkmans with no tape in them and bang our heads around till the teacher notices. When they ask what we're listening to, we tell them 'Nothing', which just drives them crazy – specially when they find out it's true!

Reports
School reports are wonderful for:
• Making bedding for your hamster or gerbil or rabbit.
• Burning.

They are not much use for anything else. Years ago reports were easy to lose on the way home from school, but these days they come with all kinds of built-in security systems, including an alarm that goes off whenever a hamster or a flame comes close to them.

But do not despair, because there is a way you can make sure of getting a reasonable report. If you think a teacher is going to say something horrible about you and there's a space for you to give your comments about the teacher, write something critical about their teaching. They hate this because they don't want your parents or guardians to think they're bad teachers. So then you can negotiate. If the teacher agrees to drop anything unfair, you can agree to drop your comment. Then everybody's happy! (*Oh no they're not! Teacher.*)

RE Teachers

RE teachers are the best people to go to when you've done something terrible at school. They are nice and holy and they believe in love and forgiveness, so if you want to confess a sin like breaking a window, go to them. If your RE teacher is not a nice, holy person, you can wind them up by asking why not.

Road Safety

The safest way of crossing the road is in a crowd. When a driver sees 200 kids running across the road he just has to stop. And even if he doesn't put his brakes on in time, only a few people will get squashed. **Warning:** there are some drivers who seem to like running school-kids over. Do not cross the road in front of them. You can tell which ones they are, because they're either talking on their mobile phones, or have fallen asleep after a big lunch.

Rubbish

Some people think it's really cool to drop their rubbish on the floor, but we don't. We hide it, so it's a surprise for someone when they find it later. We put our litter carefully away in school drawers, cupboards, desks, teacher's handbag – anywhere where a half-eaten jam sandwich will give

someone a nice shock when they find it in three
years' time.

At some schools you have to do litter duty and
collect ten bits of litter in the playground each
break-time. You see lots of wallies wandering
around searching for bits of paper and cans. Don't
they realize the place to find litter is in the bin? If
we ever have to do litter duty we just go to the
bin and get our ten bits!

Satchels

Only wallies carry satchels. And only total
plonkers carry *new* satchels. If you've got a new
satchel, kick it around in the playground for a few
weeks until it's nicely battered. If you want to be
cool like us, you'll need a rucksack. Some mothers
insist that their kids carry school gear in satchels.
The best thing to do, if you've got this kind of
mother, is to carry a rucksack in your satchel and
put the satchel in the rucksack when you get out
of the house.

Sick

If you're going to be sick in class then please throw
up over something useful! Don't just stand there and
go 'bleeeurgh' into the waste-paper basket or over
your own shoes. Aim at someone's homework book
or at the teacher or at the chemistry experiment
you're doing! This way you'll cause lots of disruption
and it'll be ages before the lesson can go on.

Some teachers are more scared of sick than

others. You can find out who are the scared ones
by going pale and saying to them, 'I feel sick.' If
they scream or run out of the room, they're
scared. You can really wind them up by feeling
sick every time you go into their class-room! (*You
horrible, horrible children! If you feel sick in class,
kids, do let me know in plenty of time so I can get
out of your way. Teacher.*)
**Also worth looking up DESPERATE
MEASURES.**

Smells

A good smell is a brilliant way of having fun in class. Bottom burps are the best sort, specially the really stinky ones that mean everyone has to leave the room. Stink bombs do the same thing, but you get into trouble if you're caught with one.

Other smells have strange effects on teachers. The nice, clean smell of washing-powder like Radion and Ariel make some teachers think you're a nice, clean kid even if you haven't washed or done any homework for weeks. We dab a few drops of Radion behind our ears before we go to school every day.

We've also found that if you cover yourself from head to foot in Lynx or Opium or Poison or something else really lovely, teachers keep their distance and don't come too close to check your work, so you don't have to do any. Easy, innit?
Also worth looking up BOTTOM BURPS.

Sponsorship

Every year at most schools there's some kind of sponsored event to raise money to buy a new coffee machine for the teachers or new blackboard dusters. This drives everyone crazy because:

1. None of the kids wants to do the event.
2. No one wants to give them any money for doing it.

We have come up with the answer. Write down all the names of the kids in a list. The person at the top of the list sponsors the second person for 10p. The second person sponsors the third person for 10p. And so on, down the list. You all do the event. The person at the top of the list pays their 10p to the second person, who pays it to the next person, and so on. Eventually a grand total of 10p is raised, no one except the person at the top of the list has had to pay any money, and everyone's happy because there'll never be another sponsored event at your school! PS Never ask a teacher to sponsor you. It will embarrass them, because they don't earn enough money to pay you.

Sports Day

Sports Day is an unofficial school holiday for us because we never go. If we're forced to take part in a race, we do the cross-country run. We don't actually run the course, of course. We're not that stupid. We just jog along slowly and when everyone's overtaken us we either catch a bus back to school or take the short cut and hang around in the bushes until we see the other runners racing home. Then we join in at the back. If you're cheating like this, don't pretend to win the race. The person who's been leading makes a terrible fuss about it.

Spots

Look up **ZITS**.

Swot

You can always tell a swot because they stagger around school trying to carry a brief-case full of 250 $3\frac{1}{2}$-inch computer disks, all with neat labels.

They are also the only kids who wear full school uniform, including grey socks. They usually wear glasses because doing so much reading and writing and staring at their computer screens has made them almost blind. They are also very pale, because they are too busy in the library or computer room to go out at break-time, and they spend all their spare time in their bedrooms writing essays and playing computer games. As they don't do anything except work, they are terribly boring. Never talk to a swot for more than two minutes, otherwise you might die of the boredom. (*Now this sounds like the kind of kid I really like! Teacher.*)
Also worth looking up IDIOTS and WALLIES.

Talking Back
Talking back really winds up teachers and makes them incredibly mad – but only if you do it properly, like we do. Most kids make the fatal mistake of trying to be cheeky, but we're always very calm and cool, and we try to keep a little smile on our face as if we don't know what the fuss is about. This makes the teacher absolutely berserk! Next time a teacher yells, 'What do you think you're doing?' at you, tell them what you're doing very politely. The teacher will just get madder and madder, until they eventually explode and have to be taken away in a bucket. Brilliant, innit?

Teachers

There are three main types of teacher:

1. The dangerous loonies. These teachers are very neat and tidy and wear shiny shoes. They also spit when they talk. If they teach computing, you will need to have windscreen wipers on your screen. Dangerous loonies have strangely glittering eyes and neat white shirts and blouses. Do not argue with them, just keep out of their way.

2. Doormats. Doormats usually look a bit sad and droopy. They sometimes button up their shirts and cardigans wrongly. They never laugh and they usually start shaking whenever they see a

kid. It's very easy to wind them up and make them cry, but it's also pretty boring, too.

3. Safe teachers. Safe teachers are rare because they're pretty normal. They usually treat kids like human beings and they have a good laugh with you in class. They can wind kids up just as much as the kids wind them up. They get angry, but they try to be fair. These are the teachers whose lessons you should go to, cos they need all the help they can get. (m r s⌐)

Trainers

Trainers are banned from most schools and you have to be careful not to get yours confiscated. We've solved the problem, though. We wear our trainers all day, every day, even in bed. They're now so wonderfully smelly that no teacher dares to confiscate them because that would mean keeping them in their desk – and the pong is just too horrible!

Also worth looking up ARMPITS, BOOTS and HALITOSIS.

Trusty

A trusty is a reliable, sensible kid who teachers use to run messages, go on errands and do all sorts of jobs around the school. Being a trusty might seem a bit boring to you and me, but trusties always know exactly what's going on. They know which teachers are going out together, who's in trouble with the head teacher and all the latest gossip. Because everyone trusts them and knows they'd never get into trouble, they can also play amazing tricks on people.
Also worth looking up GOSSIP and INVISIBILITY.

Tuck-shop

Have things changed at your school tuck-shop recently? It may have been taken over by the Tafia, an illegal organization dedicated to tuck-shop corruption. Already thousands of American school tuck-shops have been infiltrated by Tafia members, and now they're out to take over in Britain. You will know if the Tafia have arrived in your school because suddenly the price of a Mars Bar will go up to £5 and all the sweets will be past their sell-by dates. All the cans of drink will be dented, too. There is nothing you can do about this. If you try to boycott the shop the Tafia members will rough you up and force you to buy Tizer and ancient Curly Wurlies. You could try complaining to your head teacher, but if he's suddenly started wearing a dark suit and carrying a violin case, he is probably already part of the Firm. Our advice: get expelled and find a new school.

TV

The thing about schools' television programmes is that no one ever learns anything from them. Teachers just put them on when they're feeling too lazy to teach a proper lesson. The TV comes in useful on the last day of term so you can watch videos. Handy hint: put your copy of *Chainsaw Murder on Elm Street 14* in a *Bambi* box. This way teacher will think you're watching some yeuky film and stay away, allowing you and your friends to have a good time.

UFOs

UFOs are Unidentified Frying Objects. They include things like spam fritters, giant cod balls, cutlets,

doughnuts and anything dipped in breadcrumbs and fried. All these things look the same and taste pretty much the same too. Just be careful you don't put tomato sauce on your doughnuts – although, come to think of it, it wouldn't make much difference.

Also worth looking up DINNER.

Unconsciousness

Not many people know that unconsciousness can be brought on just by listening to a very boring lesson. The victim becomes glassy-eyed and just sits looking into the distance and saying nothing. Teachers call this 'not paying attention', but we know it's real unconsciousness.

Unconsciousness also happens on the cricket and rounders pitches if you let a ball get too close to your head. This is why you should always run away from balls.

Underwear

The kind of underwear you wear says a lot about you. If, for example, you wear ancient grey undies held together with safety-pins, we can tell that you're a slob.

If you wear brilliant orange or purple undies, we can tell you're either an idiot or a wally.

If you wear Teddy Ruxpin or Postman Pat underwear, you shouldn't be reading this book.

If you wear hand-knitted tie-dyed undies, you are a vegetarian hippie and probably worry a lot about the environment.

If you wear boxer shorts or Calvin Klein Y-fronts, you're cool.

If you're a girl and you wear boxer shorts, you're very strange!

If you wear black lacy knickers, you're a bit stupid. We mean, black lace for *school*?

When teachers are getting really heavy and bossy with us we find it helps if we try to imagine what kind of underwear *they're* wearing. Try it – though don't laugh too much or you'll get into even deeper trouble!

Uniform

School uniforms provide kids with an endless outlet for their creativity. You can find hundreds of different ways of adapting the rules without actually breaking them. For example, your school rules may insist that you wear a tie, but do they say how long it has to be? You can pass many happy hours trying to tie your tie shorter than anyone else's.

Your uniform makes it easy for people to identify the school you go to when you're out in the street. If you're up to something daring and you don't want to get reported to the school, we suggest you have a flexible badge on your blazer. Just sew the top edge of the badge in place, leaving the rest hanging. When you want to disguise yourself, just take off your tie and flip your school badge up and tuck it into the pocket. Now you can run around the shopping centre and no one will know which school you're from!

University

Everyone wants us to go to university but we're not going. We've heard the essays are even longer than school ones!

Also worth looking up OXFORD.

Vampires

As well as the school spirit, many schools have

dAddY

their own vampire. Vampires usually disguise themselves as kids, so see if you've got one in your class. Is there a kid who always sits at the back of the class, away from the windows, and always looks very sleepy? Does he or she cheer up in the winter, when it gets dark earlier? Do they always have what look like tomato-sauce sandwiches for lunch? Do they hate going to the dentist? If the answer to all these questions is yes, they may well be a vampire. The crucial test is to show them a mirror. If you can see their reflection in it, they're just a bit dopey. If there's no reflection you'd better have the garlic-flavoured crisps handy!

Verrucas

Verrucas are wonderful warty things that grow on the bottom of your feet. They are wonderful because if you've got one you don't have to go swimming and you can get out of PE if you're lucky. If you keep complaining that your verruca hurts, you might be allowed to wear trainers at school instead of ordinary shoes. To catch a verruca, go to the swimming-pool and walk around the changing-rooms. If you don't catch one, you can fake it by cutting a Rice Krispie in half and sticking it on the bottom of your foot. It should fool most PE teachers!

Volunteering

When a teacher asks, 'Are there any volunteers?'

you should immediately go into hiding. Volunteering for anything at school is dangerous. Teachers are lazy. If they can get kids to do something for them, they'll use them. Have you noticed that when teachers explain why they need volunteers they only tell you the good part of the task? They say, 'Any volunteers to come to the library with me and shift a few books?' and it's only when you get there you find that there are ten tonnes of encyclopaedias to move? Well, remember to keep your hands in your pockets next time they ask for volunteers!

Wallies

The thing about wallies is they try too hard and always get things wrong. They have all the latest clothes and gear, but they look a bit stupid in them. They've got all the latest dance music, but they can't dance. They think they're part of the in-crowd, but they don't realize that no one likes them. You know the kind of people we're talking about, don't you? But don't look at us like that. Wallies are useful!

They're useful because they're so anxious to be friends that they'll do things no sane person would do. Like putting a potato up the head teacher's car exhaust or phoning up the school and pretending to be your mother. We get wallies to help us out all the time, and when they get caught it doesn't really matter because the teachers know they're just wallies and aren't too tough on them.

Wellington Boots
The best thing that can be said about wellington

boots is that if you're desperate you can go to the loo in them. The only other thing to say about wellingtons is never, ever wear them unless you want to be a total prat. We know how difficult it is to get your mother to believe that no one wears them but please try.

In snowy weather you must always come to school in the lightest, silliest shoes you can find. Slippers would be good and so would summer sandals. By the time you get to school your feet will be so cold and wet the teachers will immediately send you home again. Clever, aren't we?

Xs
Bad news. All those Xs on your work do not mean teacher is madly in love with you. They mean you're stupid.

Yellow
We haven't ever seen any kids wearing yellow school blazers. Green, blue, black, red, even orange – but never yellow. Why not, we'd like to know? Yellow is a very practical colour for school blazers. At least the custard stains wouldn't show!

Zebra Crossings
Do not use zebra crossings. The minute car drivers see a kid on a zebra crossing they go

mad and try to run them over. At least, that's what happens when they see *us*.

Also worth looking up ROAD SAFETY.

Zen

Zen is one type of Buddhism, and Buddhism involves sitting still and meditating with your eyes closed. So next time you're having a quiet snooze in the class-room and a teacher accuses you of being asleep, tell them that you're a Zen Buddhist and were just meditating. With a bit of luck they'll be so impressed that you'll get away with it.

Zero

Zero in your exams is a mark to be really proud

of. We've never achieved this magnificent score because at our schools we always get one mark for sitting down at the desk and another for putting our names on the paper, even if we don't spell them properly. The only way we know of to get zero in an exam is not to turn up at all – and that would be cheating!

Zits
Look up **SPOTS**.

Zoo
The zoo is a good place for school outings. We really like the monkeys, because they're always doing naughty things to each other and we make the teacher go red by asking them to explain what they're up to!

You must take care at the zoo. Some zoo keepers don't like kids running round and shouting and waking up all their boring old animals. So if a keeper asks you if you'd like a closer look at the lions we'd advise you to run like crazy or risk getting eaten.